Pebble Plus

T0061187

A Visit to The Doctor's Office

Revised Edition

4D

Download the Capstone 4D app for additional content.

See page 2 for directions.

by Blake A. Hoena

CAPSTONE PRESS
a capstone imprint

Download the Capstone 4D app!

- Ask an adult to search in the Apple App Store or Google Play for "Capstone 4D".
- Click Install (Android) or Get, then Install (Apple).
- Open the app.
- Scan any of the following spreads with this icon:

When you scan a spread, you'll find fun extra stuff to go with this book!
You can also find these things on the web at www.capstone4D.com
using the password: **doctor.08277**

Pebble Plus is published by Capstone Press,
1710 Roe Crest Drive, North Mankato, Minnesota 56003
www.mycapstone.com

Copyright © 2018 by Capstone Press, a Capstone imprint.
All rights reserved. No part of this publication may be reproduced in whole or in part, or stored in a retrieval system, or transmitted in any form or by any means, electronic, mechanical, photocopying, recording, or otherwise, without written permission of the publisher

Library of Congress Cataloging-in-Publication Data
is available on the Library of Congress website.

ISBN 978-1-5435-0827-7 (library binding)
ISBN 978-1-5435-0839-0 (paperback)
ISBN 978-1-5435-0867-3 (ebook pdf)

Editorial Credits
Sarah Bennett, designer; Tracy Cummins, media researcher; Laura Manthe, production specialist

Photo Credits
Capstone Press: Gary Sundermeyer, Cover Left, 7, 11, 13, 17, 19; Getty Images: Thomas Barwick, 15; iStockphoto: andresr, 21, fotografixx, 9, RichLegg, 5; Shutterstock: amirage, Design Element, PhotoSerg, Cover Background

Note to Parents and Teachers

The A Visit to set supports national social studies standards related to the production, distribution, and consumption of goods and services. This book describes and illustrates a doctor's office. The images support early readers in understanding the text. The repetition of words and phrases helps early readers learn new words. This book also introduces early readers to subject-specific vocabulary words, which are defined in the Glossary section. Early readers may need assistance to read some words and to use the Table of Contents, Glossary, Read More, Internet Sites, Critical Thinking Questions, and Index sections of the book.

Printed in the United States 3958

Table of Contents

The Doctor's Office 4

Around the Office 8

The Exam Room 14

The Lab 18

Staying Healthy. 20

Glossary 22

Read More. 23

Internet Sites 23

Critical Thinking Questions 24

Index 24

The Doctor's Office

A doctor's office is a busy place to visit. People go to the doctor's office when they are sick or need a checkup.

People sit in the waiting room.

They wait to see

a doctor or a nurse.

ANSEL A
Light

Around the Office

Office workers keep records
and make appointments.
They file charts and answer
the phones.

Nurses help patients get ready
to see a doctor.
Nurses write down how
much each patient weighs.

Health o meter

Doctors write prescriptions

and read charts.

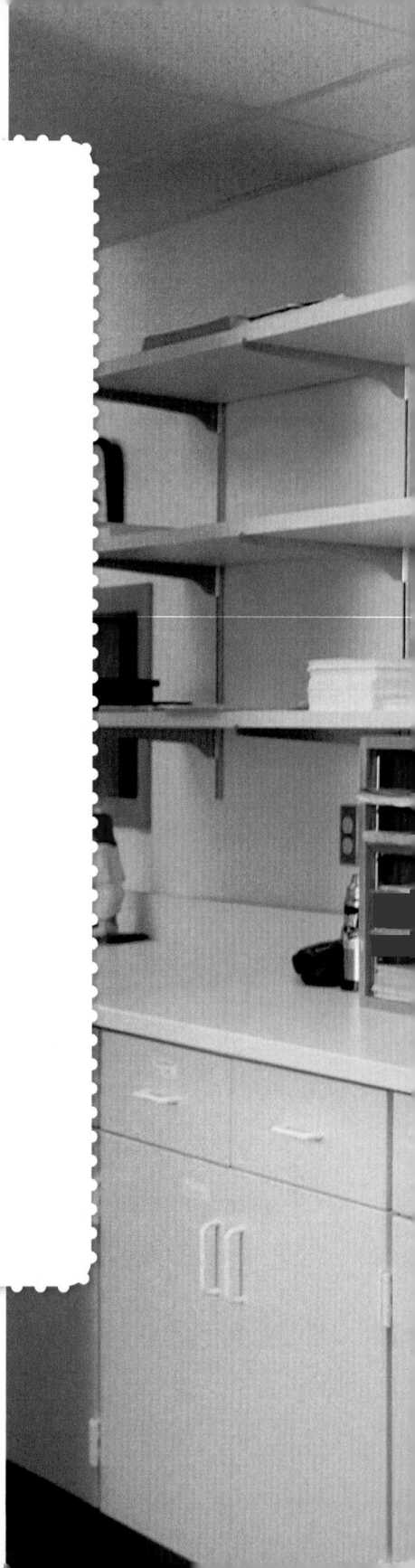

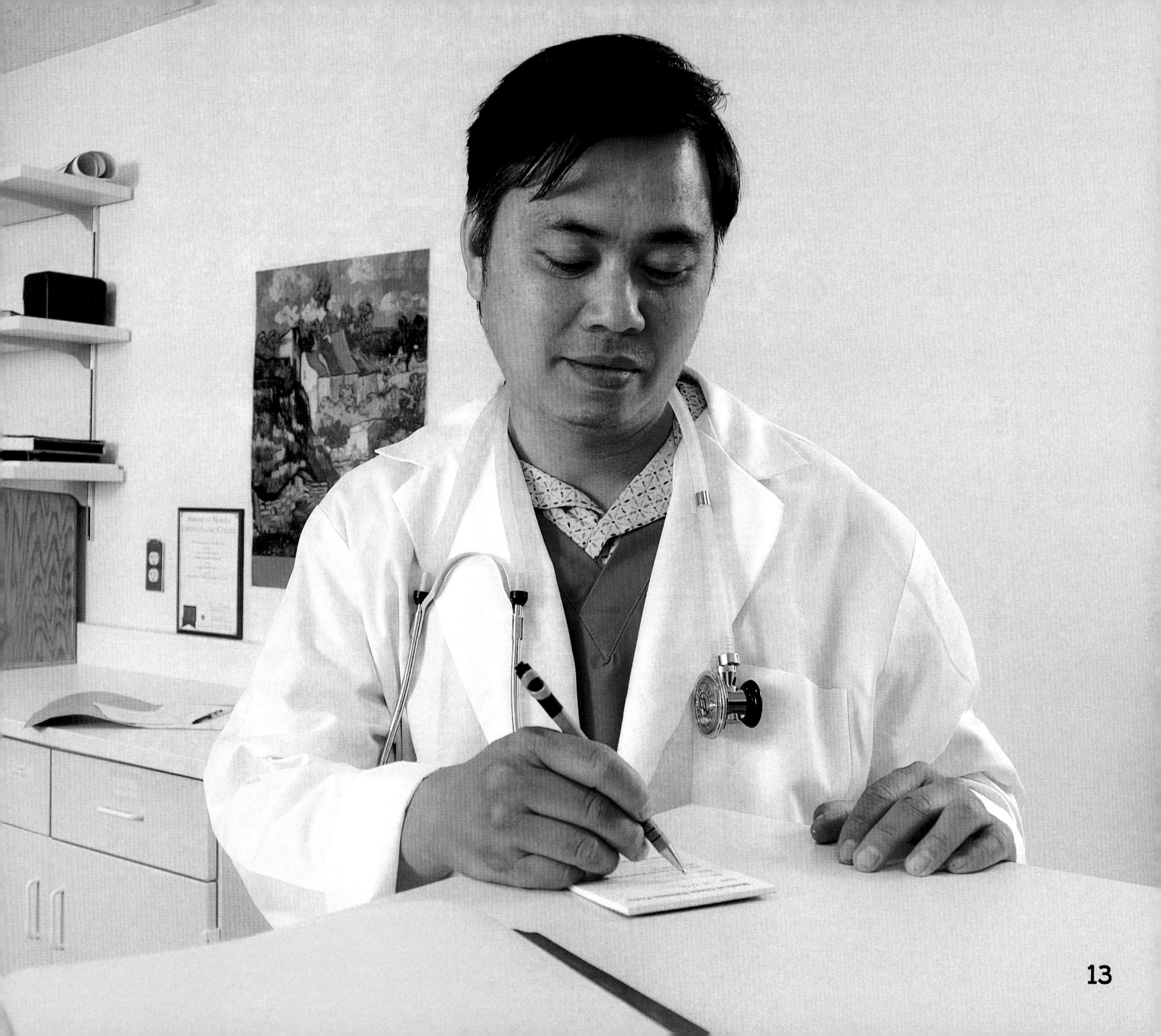

The Exam Room

Patients see their doctor
in the exam room.
The patient sits on a table
during an exam.

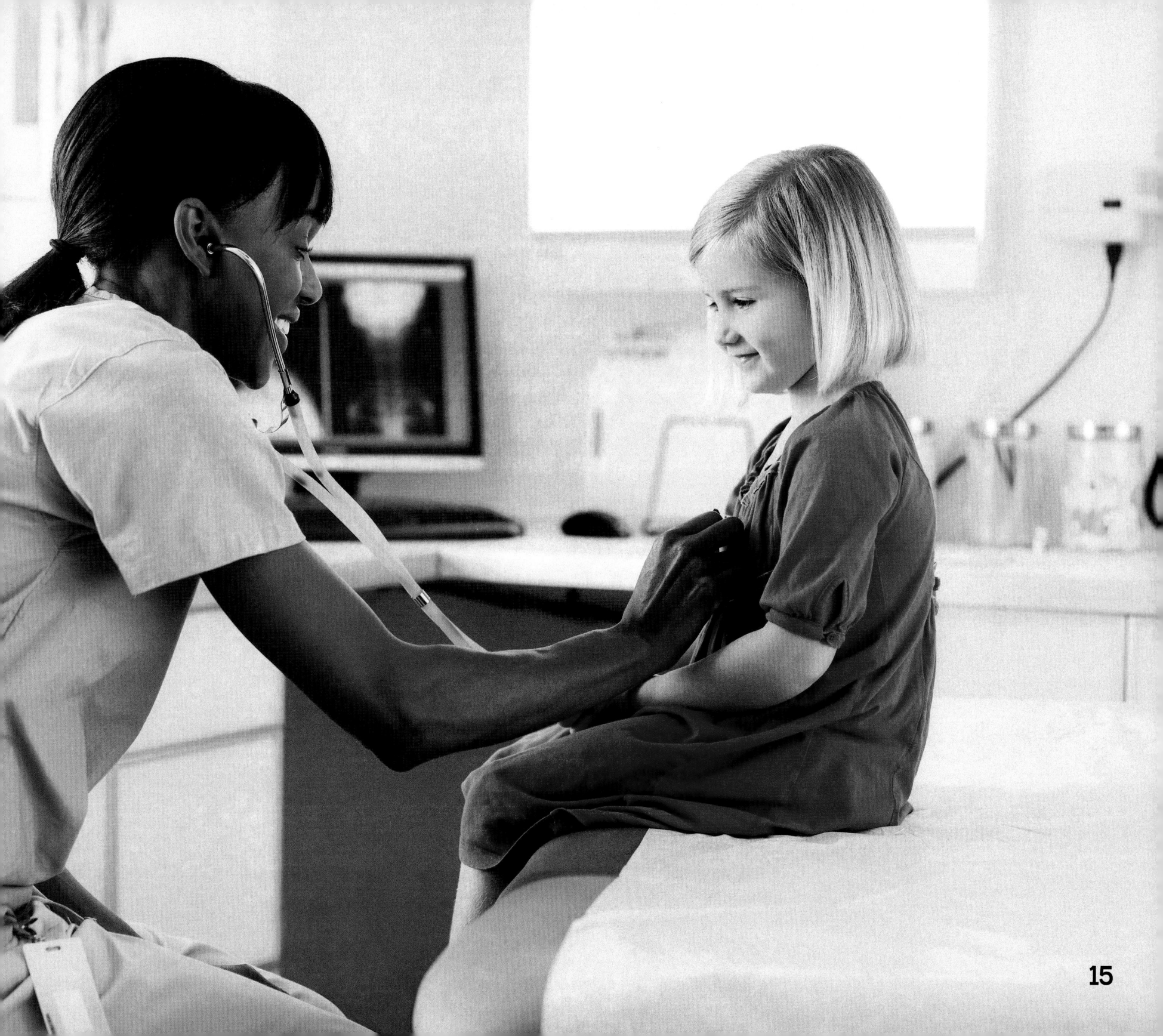

Instruments help doctors

and nurses check their patients.

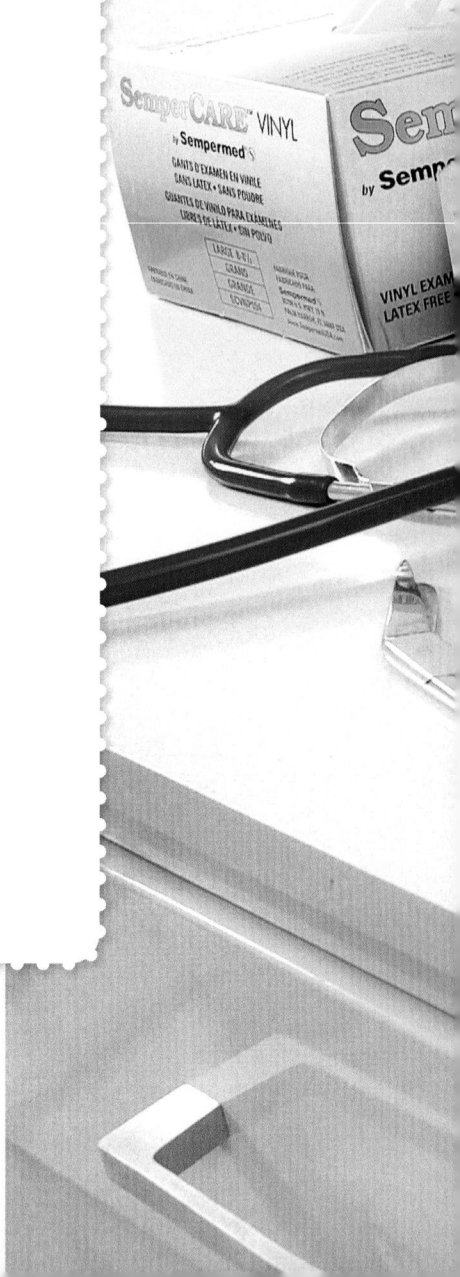

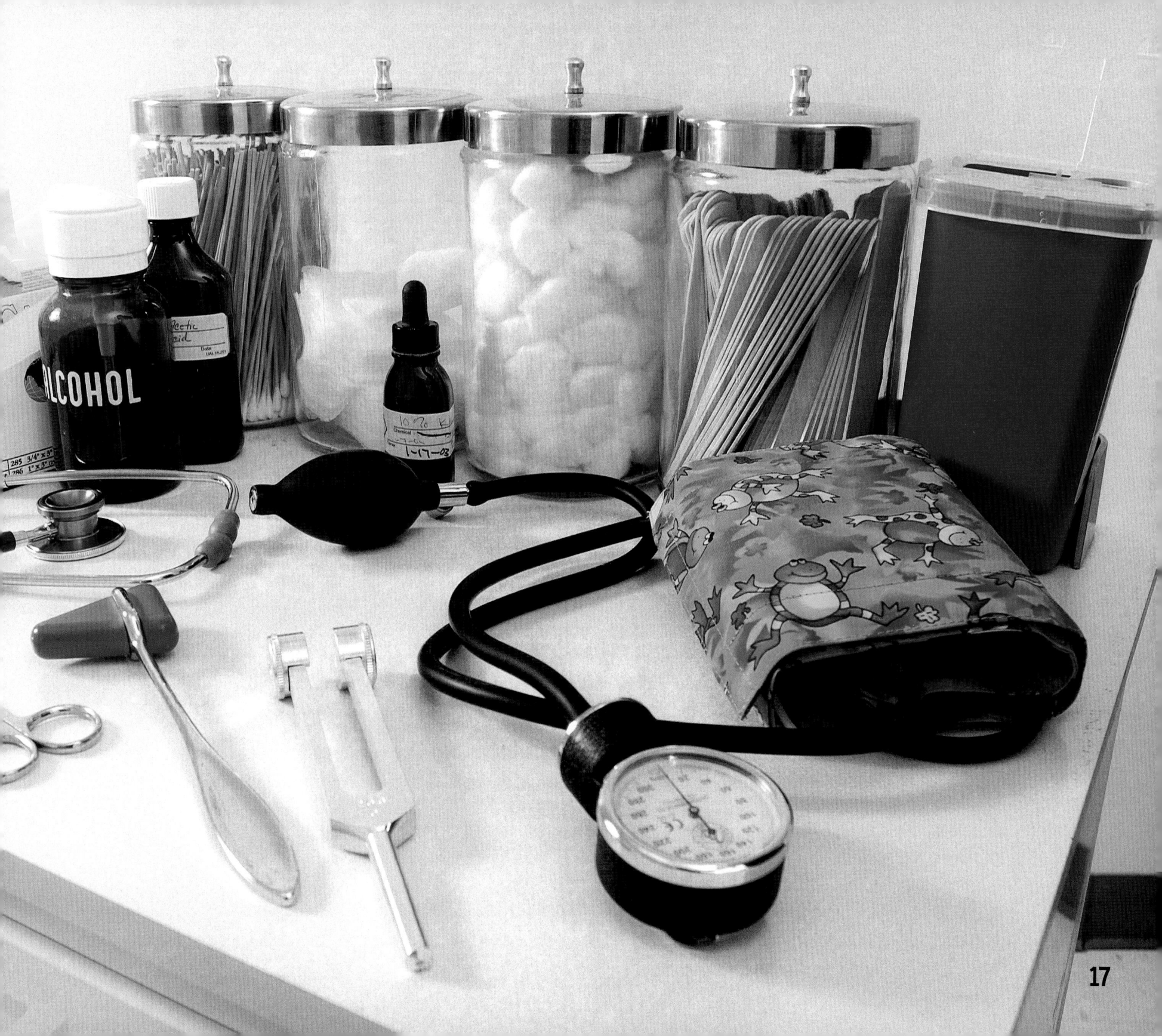
ALCOHOL
1-17-03

The Lab

Lab workers do tests in the lab.
Gloves keep their hands
clean and safe.

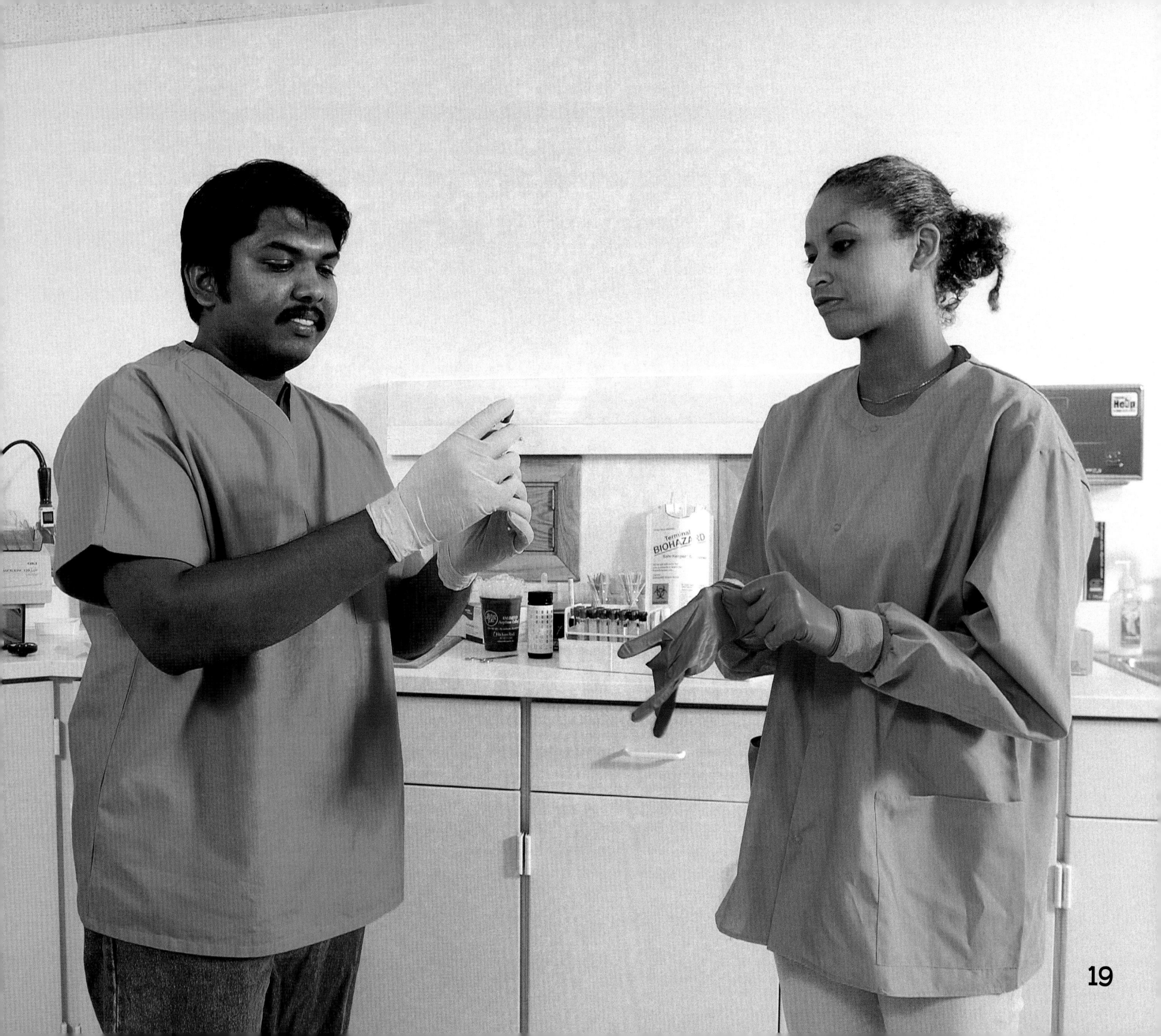
Terminal
BIOHAZARD

Staying Healthy

People visit the doctor's office
to help them feel better
and stay healthy.

Glossary

appointment—an arrangement to meet someone at a certain time

chart—the place where information about a patient is kept; information is added to a chart each time a patient visits the doctor's office

exam room—a room where doctors and nurses check the health of a patient; another word for exam is examination

instrument—a medical tool used to examine or treat patients

lab—a room with equipment that is used to do scientific tests; another word for lab is laboratory

patient—a person who is cared for by a doctor or a nurse

prescription—a written order for medicine

Read More

Bellamy, Adam. *This Is My Doctor.* All About My World. New York: Enslow Publishing, 2017.

Kenan, Tessa. *Hooray for Doctors!* Hooray for Community Helpers! Minneapolis: Lerner Publications, 2018.

Siemens, Jared. *The Doctor.* People in My Neighborhood. New York: Smartbook Media, Inc., 2018.

Internet Sites

Use FactHound to find Internet sites related to this book.

Visit *www.facthound.com*

Just type 9781543508277 and go.

Critical Thinking Questions

1. What do lab workers wear to stay safe?

2. Describe what nurses do.

3. Do you like going to the doctor's office? Why or why not?

Index

answer, 8
appointments, 8
charts, 8, 12
checkup, 4
clean, 18
doctors, 4, 6, 10, 12, 14, 16, 20
exam, 14
exam room, 14
file, 8
gloves, 18
healthy, 20
help, 10, 16, 20
instruments, 16
lab, 18
nurses, 6, 10, 16
office workers, 8
patient, 10, 14, 16
phones, 8
prescriptions, 12
records, 8
safe, 18
sick, 4
tests, 18
visit, 4, 20
waiting room, 6